THE EXCURSIONIST OF AN UNMAPPED ROAD

SUHA

Contents

1

The Path Less Travelled

In a world where the pressure to conform often feels suffocating, there is an undeniable beauty in choosing to forge your way. For me, the journey down this road was far more than a mere adventure. It was a bold act of defiance and a declaration of my independence. It was a decision to step away from the well-worn paths that everyone around me seemed so comfortable following. And while this new journey was filled with uncertainty and obstacles, it was also rich with self-discovery, personal growth, and endless possibilities.

Reflecting on my life, I see how growing up in an environment of love and support shaped who I was in my early years. My family provided a safety net that I could always rely on, and it gave me a sense of security that should have made life feel easy. I was blessed to have parents who encouraged me, a sister who stood by me, and a close circle of friends who admired my drive and determination. From an early age, I seemed to excel in nearly everything I did. I thrived in school, consistently earning high grades and praise from teachers. I was a perfectionist, driven by the need to achieve and be recognised for my efforts. I was also a great swimmer being able to win all school swimming competition, leading myself to numerous victories. In many ways, I was considered a role model, someone my peers could look up to.

Debating was another passion of mine. Whether in a formal competition or a casual argument with friends, I loved the thrill of crafting arguments and finding ways to make my point. I was articulate, passionate, and determined to win every debate. And so, for much of my childhood and teenage years, my identity was defined by these achievements. I was the "winner," the high achiever who could do everything.

This self-image was reinforced by a mantra I had adopted early on: "Winning isn't everything; it's the only thing." I took this belief to heart, allowing it to guide my every move. Winning meant validation. It meant admiration. It meant proof that I was on the right path. I poured myself into every competition, whether a swim race, an academic test, or a debate. I pushed myself to achieve excellence, to ensure that every step I took was leading me closer to success. Every victory, every accolade, felt like a confirmation that I was doing things right.

But despite my success, a small voice inside me began to whisper doubts. As much as winning fuelled my ambition, it also started to sow the seeds of uncertainty. Was I winning for the right reasons? Did I truly love the challenges I was taking on, or was I merely seeking the approval of others? I found myself questioning the very foundations of my motivations. The constant drive for success became exhausting. My victories no longer brought the same joy, and I began to feel a strange disconnect between my outer achievements and my inner self.

In the quiet moments, when there was no one to impress and no competition to win, I started to feel a sense of emptiness. I was following a script written by society, excelling at it, but I couldn't shake the feeling that something was missing.

The path I was on seemed predetermined, mapped out by societal expectations and the desires of those around me. I had been so focused on winning that I had never stopped to ask myself if this was the life I truly wanted.

That was when the idea of taking the path less traveled first entered my mind. It wasn't a sudden epiphany but rather a slow, dawning realisation that my life, despite its outward success, was starting to feel hollow. I was moving forward, yes, but I wasn't sure where I was going. The pressure to maintain my image as a winner, as someone who had it all together, weighed heavily on me. I realised that I was no longer enjoying the journey I was on, and the destination I was heading toward no longer seemed appealing.

The turning point came when I began to ask myself some of the hardest questions I had ever faced. What did I want out of life? What was my purpose beyond the trophies, accolades, and recognition I had collected? The answers didn't come easily, and sometimes, they were uncomfortable. But as difficult as it was, I knew that I needed to step off the well-beaten track if I ever wanted to find the answers. I needed to redefine success for myself, to take control of my narrative. This realisation was both terrifying and exhilarating. I knew that by choosing this path, I would likely disappoint some people and would have to let go of the carefully crafted image I had built for myself.

And so, with a mixture of fear and excitement, I decided to venture into the unknown. I chose to take the path less traveled. It was not an easy decision, and the journey that followed was even harder. I had to give up some of the things that had once been integral to my identity. I stepped down from the swimming team, not because I no longer loved the sport, but because I needed to make space for new experiences.

I stopped participating in debates, choosing instead to explore conversations without the pressure of always needing to be right. It felt like I was shedding a skin that no longer fit me. And in doing so, I felt both liberated and vulnerable.

During this period of transition, I came face to face with one of my greatest fears: failure. For so long, I had avoided failure at all costs, associating it with weakness and inadequacy. But now, on this new path, failure has become an essential part of my journey. The path less traveled is full of uncertainties, and there were many moments where I stumbled, doubted myself, or felt lost. But with each failure, I learned something invaluable about myself. I learned to appreciate growth over perfection, and I found joy in the process rather than focusing solely on the outcome.

Another unexpected gift of this journey was solitude. On this new path, there were fewer people to impress and fewer external expectations to meet. I had to learn to listen to my voice, a voice that had often been drowned out by the noise of others' validation. I began to pursue interests that felt more authentic to me, even if they didn't come with the same recognition or praise. I found myself drawn to writing and self-reflection, activities that allowed me to connect with my thoughts in a more meaningful way. I also started volunteering for causes that aligned with my values, not because I was seeking recognition, but because it felt like the right thing to do.

As I embraced this new way of living, the relationships in my life began to shift. Some friends didn't understand the changes I was making. They were used to the version of me that always strived for the top, the version of me that was always winning. And while their confusion and distance were painful at times, it was also part of the process.

As I embraced authenticity, I naturally gravitated toward people who supported my growth rather than my accomplishments. These new connections were built on deeper, more meaningful foundations.

In walking the path less traveled, I learned one of life's greatest lessons: that life is not a race, and success is not a destination. Life is a journey, one that is unique to each of us. The greatest victories are not the ones that come with medals or awards, but the ones that bring us closer to understanding who we truly are. It's about finding fulfilment in the moments, in the choices we make that align with our values and beliefs, rather than in the external validation we receive.

Looking back, I realise that taking the path less traveled was the most important decision I ever made. It taught me that courage is not about being fearless; it's about moving forward despite the fear. It showed me that life is not about winning at everything, but about finding meaning and fulfilment in the things that truly matter. Most importantly, it helped me see that true success is not defined by how others perceive us, but by how closely we live in alignment with our authentic selves.

There are still moments when I look back on the life I left behind and wonder how different things might have been had I stayed on that path. But I have no regrets. The path less traveled may not come with the same guarantees or applause, but it offers something far more valuable: the freedom to be yourself. And that, I have come to realise, is the greatest victory of all.

2
The Dream Shattered

During my years pursuing a bachelor's degree, I lived a life filled with quiet introspection, forming deep friendships, and excelling in my studies. I wasn't just content with doing well academically; I sought to make a mark in all areas of life. One of the highlights was winning first place in a march past. At that moment, I felt unstoppable, like life was unfolding exactly as I had planned. But life has its ways of reminding us that we are not always in control.

Anecdote

It was simply another typical day, like any other. I was heading to college, riding a public vehicle, probably lost in thoughts of the future that seemed so promising. Then, in the blink of an eye, my world turned upside down—literally. I fell from the vehicle and sustained a severe head injury. Everything went dark. It was as if someone had pressed pause on my life.

I don't remember much of what happened immediately after, but my family does. I learned later that for 24 agonising hours, my life hung in the balance. Doctors told my parents that I was 50% to 60% close to brain death. For 21 days, I lay in a coma, completely unaware of the world around me, disconnected from everything I had once known.

Waking up from that coma was not the relief you might imagine. I didn't snap back to consciousness and immediately recognised the familiar faces of my family or friends. Instead, everything felt distant, foreign. My mother, who had been my rock through every hardship, stood by my bedside with tear-streaked cheeks, but I couldn't even remember her name. The weight of that disorientation was immense, and it made me realise how fragile our connection to the world truly is.

Reflection

Coming to terms with the aftermath of the accident was one of the hardest things I've ever had to do. I had not only lost memories; I felt like I had lost myself. The vibrant, ambitious person I had once been was now a shadow, struggling to piece together fragments of a life that felt unfamiliar. The sharpness of my mind, the sense of invincibility I had clung to, and the dreams I had nurtured—they all seemed so far away.

What does one do when faced with the reality that life may never be the same again? How do you cope when everything you've worked for feels like it's slipping through your fingers? The initial days after waking up were filled with confusion and frustration. I wanted so desperately to remember, to reclaim the identity I had lost. But the truth was, I had to accept that the life I knew was forever changed.

That realisation—that acceptance—was not easy. But in that space of loss, I began to understand something deeper about life. I had always defined myself by my achievements, by how well I was doing in school, by how many trophies I won, by how successful I seemed on the outside. But now, stripped of those external markers, I was left with only myself. And I had to ask, "Who am I? What does success look like when the world I knew is gone?"

Lesson

Life, I have come to understand, can change in an instant. One moment, everything seems to be going according to plan, and in the next, the ground beneath you shifts, and you're left grappling with an entirely new reality. But here's the thing: life's unpredictability doesn't just bring pain or loss. It also brings growth. Sometimes, it's in those darkest, most uncertain moments that we find the strength we never knew we had.

In my case, I had to relearn how to appreciate the little victories—like remembering a loved one's face or regaining the ability to recall small moments from my past. I had to embrace the unknown, understanding that I might never be the same person I was before the accident. But perhaps that's the point. Perhaps life isn't about clinging to who we used to be or what we used to achieve. Instead, it's about evolving, even when the path ahead seems uncertain.

The biggest lesson I've learned from this experience is that resilience isn't about bouncing back to who you were. It's about forging a new path with the pieces you have left. It's about learning to thrive, not despite the challenges, but because of them.

I now understand that our true strength lies not in our ability to control life, but in our ability to adapt to it. There will be moments in all of our lives when things don't go as planned. When we are forced to face the unknown, it feels terrifying. But those are the moments that shape us, that reveal the depths of our courage and resilience.

Looking back, I see that the accident, while tragic, was also a turning point in my life. It taught me that success isn't about external achievements—it's about inner growth. It's about who we become in the face of adversity and how we choose to move forward when the world as we know it is shattered.

So, if I could leave you with one piece of advice, it would be this: Life will throw challenges your way. There will be moments when everything falls apart, and you're left questioning who you are and where you're going. In those moments, don't focus on trying to put the pieces back together exactly as they were. Instead, embrace the change, trust in your strength, and know that, even in the darkness, there is always a way forward.

The path may be different from the one you envisioned, but it's still your path. And with every step you take, you'll discover more about who you truly are—and that, I believe, is the greatest success of all.

3

Awakening to a New Reality — A Journey of Rediscovery

Waking up after a traumatic accident is not the same as simply opening your eyes to a new day. For me, it felt like waking up in a world that no longer recognised me, and worse, a world I no longer recognised. Everything I once knew, the reality I once held dear, was gone. My mind, once sharp and filled with memories, now struggled to even grasp the simplest of tasks. I wasn't just waking up from an accident. I was waking up to a new life – a second life.

When I first opened my eyes in the hospital, the faces around me were both familiar and strange. I saw my family, their expressions a mix of relief and overwhelming sadness, but their names and roles in my life were blurry. I knew they were important to me, but in those early days, I couldn't fully connect the dots. My father, who had always been my source of strength, decided to take me back to my hometown after I was discharged, hoping that the familiarity of the environment would help me regain the pieces of my past. He believed that by surrounding me with the places and things I once loved, my memories might slowly return.

Anecdote

One day, in an attempt to trigger some sense of familiarity, I decided to visit a place that used to be incredibly special to me as a child: a park named Adhere Park in my country. This park had been a sanctuary of joy for me during my early years. I had spent countless evenings there, playing on the swings, running through the sand, and laughing with friends. It was a place filled with warmth and innocence. But when I returned to Adhere Park this time, something felt off. It was as though I was a ghost walking through the remnants of someone else's life.

I watched as children played on the swings, their laughter ringing out in the air, but instead of feeling comforted, I felt disconnected. It was painful. The park, once vibrant with memories, felt like a reminder of everything I had lost. I saw familiar faces—people I once knew, friends who had been a part of my life before the accident—but they had all moved on. They were living in the present, while I was stuck in a fog of lost memories. It was as though I had been dropped into someone else's life, a life that I could no longer fully access or understand.

I wanted to feel something—some spark of recognition, some connection to my old self—but instead, I felt like a stranger in my past. That realisation hit me harder than any physical pain I had experienced during my recovery. It was a different kind of pain, one that ran deep into the core of my being. At that moment, I realised that the life I had before the accident, the life filled with memories and familiar routines, was truly gone. And I had to face the fact that I might never fully get it back.

Reflection

This was the start of what would become one of the greatest challenges of my life. The journey of healing and rediscovery was not going to be straightforward. I had imagined that waking up from the accident would mean slowly but steadily returning to who I had been before. But life isn't like that. Healing, I learned, is not a straight line. It's a winding path with peaks of hope and valleys of despair. One day, I would make progress, and the next, it would feel like I was back at square one.

As I walked through that park, I couldn't help but reflect on how much had changed. My friends had moved on. While I was struggling to remember the most basic things, they were forging ahead with their lives, making new memories, and building their futures. I, on the other hand, felt stuck in a past I could barely remember. It was as though I was frozen in time while the world kept spinning around me.

But in those quiet moments of reflection, I began to understand something important. Life wasn't going to wait for me. I had to choose whether I would remain stuck in the past, mourning the loss of my old self, or whether I would move forward and begin to embrace this second chance at life, no matter how different it was from the life I had planned.

Lesson

What I learned in that park, and in the weeks and months that followed, is that reconnecting with oneself is one of the hardest but most important journeys we can undertake. I had to accept that the person I was before the accident was gone. And in accepting that, I had to give myself the grace and the time to discover who I was becoming. This wasn't just about healing my physical injuries or regaining my memories. It was about rebuilding my identity from the ground up.

I allowed myself to feel the full weight of my emotions—the sadness, the frustration, the anger at how unfair it all felt. I stopped trying to force myself to be the person I once was and instead started focusing on the person I am now. Reconnecting with yourself, especially after a traumatic event, is not easy. There will be moments when it feels impossible when the gap between who you were and who you are feels too wide to bridge. But it's in those moments that you need to be kind to yourself.

I learned to celebrate the small victories. When I could finally remember a detail about my past, no matter how insignificant, it was a triumph. When I began to feel more comfortable in my skin, even if I wasn't the same as before, it was progress. Healing doesn't happen all at once; it happens in small steps. Each day, I moved a little further from the darkness of my past and a little closer to the light of my new reality.

Life doesn't always go according to plan. Sometimes, it shatters in ways we never could have anticipated. But even in those moments, when everything feels lost, there is always the opportunity to rebuild. And sometimes, what we build after the storm is stronger, more resilient, and more beautiful than what came before.

I now see that my accident, while devastating, gave me a second chance at life—a second chance to rediscover myself, redefine my priorities, and find new meaning in the world around me. I am grateful with no counts for being blessed with another chance in life while still being able to talk, walk, see & feel everything like any other Human does. The world may not be the same as it was before, but neither am I. And in that, I've found a new strength, a strength that comes not from the things I've lost, but from the person I've become.

4

The Long Road to Recovery — A Journey of Perseverance and Growth

Recovery isn't a straight line. It twists, turns, and sometimes doubles back, making it one of the most challenging paths one can walk. After my accident, I knew I had a long road ahead, but nothing could prepare me for just how steep that climb would be. The process of physical and cognitive therapy felt like an endless journey up a mountain I wasn't sure I could conquer. Yet, every day I showed up, determined to keep going, no matter how slow my progress seemed.

Anecdote

One moment that stands out vividly from that time was a particularly tough day during one of my therapy sessions. My therapist had given me a simple puzzle to solve—something that a few years prior would have been easy. But in that moment, it felt impossible. I struggled, staring at the pieces as if they were foreign objects. My hands trembled with the effort of trying to piece them together. The frustration was overwhelming, and I felt a deep, painful sense of loss. I wasn't just struggling with the puzzle; I was grappling with the fact that I wasn't the person I once was.

As the minutes dragged on, the weight of it all became too much, and I broke down in tears. My therapist, a kind and patient person, simply sat beside me. She didn't rush me, didn't try to push me through it. Instead, she quietly reminded me, "Every small victory counts. Every step you take is progress, no matter how insignificant it feels right now."

Those words, simple as they were, hit me like a wave of relief. I hadn't considered the steps in that way. Up until that point, I had been so focused on how far I had to go that I hadn't stopped to acknowledge how far I had already come. My therapist's words gave me the strength to keep going, to push through the frustration, and try again. The next day, when I finally completed the puzzle, it felt like I had climbed Mount Everest. It was an insignificant win, but in that moment, it felt tremendous. It wasn't just about solving the puzzle—it was about proving to myself that I could still overcome obstacles, no matter how difficult.

Reflection

Those therapy sessions were more than just physical and cognitive exercises. They were lessons in patience, perseverance, and self-compassion. Each day brought new challenges, and there were plenty of moments when I wanted to quit. But I learned that progress isn't always about making giant leaps forward. Sometimes, it's about the small, steady steps that eventually lead to something greater. Every day that I showed up for therapy, even on the days when I made little to no progress, I was building something within myself—strength, resilience, and the ability to keep moving forward even when it felt like I was stuck in place.

Through this process, I began to understand the importance of finding joy in small achievements. It was easy to get caught up in the big picture, to focus on how far I still had to go. But I learned that if I only measured success by the end goal, I would never appreciate the journey. So, I started to celebrate the little things—the first time I walked a few extra steps without feeling dizzy, the first time I remembered something on my own without help, the first time I laughed without feeling guilty for my pain. Each of these small moments became a reminder that I was still moving forward, still growing, still healing.

Lesson

One of the most valuable lessons I took from this journey was the importance of perseverance in the face of adversity. It's easy to feel defeated when progress is slow, especially when you're recovering from something that has changed your life in such a significant way. But every step forward, no matter how small, is a victory. It's a testament to your resilience, to your determination to keep moving even when the road ahead feels impossible to navigate.

I learned that recovery isn't about perfection—it's about progress. It's about showing up for yourself every day, even when it feels like nothing is changing. There were so many days when I felt like I wasn't improving at all when it felt like I was just going through the motions without getting anywhere. But every day that I showed up was a step forward, whether I realised it in the moment or not.

The key, I discovered, is to recognise and celebrate progress, even if it's just the tiniest step forward. Sometimes, the progress we make isn't visible right away. It's internal—it's the way we slowly rebuild our confidence, our strength, our ability to keep going. It's the way we learn to adapt to our new reality, to accept where we are, and to keep moving forward despite the challenges.

This journey also taught me to be kinder to myself. Before the accident, I had always been my harshest critic, always pushing myself to be better, faster, stronger. But recovery taught me that sometimes, the most important thing you can do is simply be gentle with yourself. It's okay to have bad days. It's okay to feel frustrated sad or overwhelmed. What matters is that you don't give up. What matters is that you keep going, even when it feels like you can't.

In many ways, the accident gave me a second life. It forced me to slow down, to reevaluate what truly mattered, and to find strength in places I didn't know existed. It taught me that life is full of unexpected challenges, but it's also full of opportunities for growth and resilience. It showed me that we are capable of far more than we realise, especially when we are pushed to our limits.

You know…….

The road to recovery is never easy, and it's often filled with moments of doubt, frustration, and fear. But it's also filled with moments of triumph, no matter how small they may seem. Every challenge is an opportunity to grow stronger, learn more about yourself, and build resilience that will carry you through whatever life throws your way.

For anyone facing their challenges, I want to say this: Don't give up. The road may be long, and the progress may feel slow, but every step forward is a victory. Celebrate your small wins. Be kind to yourself. And remember, the journey is just as important as the destination. It's in the struggle that we find our strength, and it's in the perseverance that we discover who we truly are.

5

A Changed Landscape — Finding My Way Back

Returning to college after my accident was a mix of exhilaration and terror. The familiar hallways, bustling with students and lively chatter, reminded me of a life I used to know. Friends would approach me, recalling the days when I was achieving so much. Their words came from a place of warmth, but to me, they felt like echoes from a distant past. It was as though I had been a different person—one who excelled effortlessly. Now, I felt like a stranger in my own life, unsure of how to reclaim what I had lost.

Anecdote

I'll never forget my first class back. It was a subject I once loved, a course where I used to actively engage in discussions, unafraid to voice my opinions. But this time, I sat in silence, feeling as though I no longer belonged. As my peers discussed the material passionately, I found myself overwhelmed by feelings of inadequacy. Each word spoken by them felt like a reminder of what I had lost, and I began to retreat further into myself.

After class, I gathered my things, preparing to leave when a friend I hadn't spoken to in months approached me. She smiled and asked,

"Hey, do you want to study together later?" That simple invitation caught me off guard. It wasn't just the words; it was the warmth behind them. For the first time in what felt like forever, someone was treating me as though I hadn't changed—as though I was still me. That small act of kindness sparked something inside me, a flicker of hope that perhaps I could find my way back, little by little.

Reflection

Loneliness had become my constant companion during this time. It would whisper doubts in my ear, telling me I didn't belong, and that I would never be the person I once was. I started to believe those thoughts. As I watched my friends move on with their lives, I felt as though I was being left behind, stuck in a version of myself that no longer existed.

But amidst this overwhelming sense of loss, something shifted. I began to understand that maybe my journey wasn't about returning to who I had been. Perhaps it was about embracing who I was becoming. I realised that my accident, while it had taken away parts of my old life, had also opened the door for something new. I just had to figure out what that was.

Writing became my refuge. Whenever I felt lost or disconnected, I would turn to my journal, letting the words flow from my heart onto the page. It was as though I was reclaiming my narrative, piece by piece. Through writing, I was able to process my emotions—the fear, the anger, the sadness—and in doing so, I began to heal.

Writing allowed me to connect with myself in ways I hadn't before. It gave me the space to explore who I was now, without the pressure of being the person everyone else expected me to be. I wrote about my frustrations, my small victories, and my dreams. Slowly but surely, I started to see that my life wasn't over just because it had changed. I was still here, still capable of growing and evolving, even if the path ahead looked different than what I had imagined.

Lesson

The greatest lesson I learned during this time was the power of creative expression in healing. Writing wasn't just an outlet for me; it became a tool that allowed me to redefine my identity. When everything felt uncertain, when I doubted whether I could move forward, my journal became a place where I could be honest with myself. It was through that process of honesty that I began to find clarity.

Each time I put pen to paper, I was reminded that I had control over my story. I may not have been able to change what had happened to me, but I could choose how I responded to it. I could choose to let it break me, or I could choose to let it shape me into someone stronger, more compassionate, and more self-aware.

Through writing, I also found a way to connect with others. I started sharing my thoughts and experiences with friends, and to my surprise, they didn't see me as someone broken. They saw me as someone brave, someone who was facing unimaginable challenges but still choosing to move forward. Their support, along with my growing confidence in myself, helped me see that I wasn't alone in this journey.

Looking back, I can say that my time in college after the accident wasn't just about returning to my studies. It was about learning to trust myself again, about finding strength in my vulnerability. I discovered that we are all capable of incredible resilience, even when we feel lost or afraid. And sometimes, that resilience comes from the most unexpected places—like a journal entry or a friend's kind words.

You know....

As I continued my journey of recovery, I learned that change, though painful, doesn't have to be the end. It can be a new beginning. The road to healing isn't easy, and it's not without its setbacks. But every small step forward is progress. Every time we choose to keep going, even when we feel like giving up, we're growing in ways we may not yet understand.

For me, writing became a way to reclaim my life. It allowed me to make sense of my pain, embrace the unknown, and find strength in my new reality. I learned that we don't have to be defined by our past achievements or our struggles. We have the power to define ourselves, to create new beginnings, and to keep moving forward, one step at a time.

No matter what you're going through, remember this: your story isn't over. You have the strength within you to keep writing new chapters, and each one holds the potential for growth, healing, and hope.

6

Embracing the Unknown

As the months passed and I continued to heal, I found myself reflecting on the very nature of life. There had been a time when the future terrified me when the weight of my past felt like an anchor holding me back. But slowly, I began to understand something important: life doesn't wait for us. It moves forward, with or without our consent, witnessing our struggles and triumphs alike. The question wasn't whether I would keep up with life's rhythm, but rather, how I would choose to experience it.

Anecdote

One quiet evening, after a long day of therapy and self-reflection, I sat under a vast starlit sky, journaling as I often did. The cool night air wrapped around me, and there was a certain stillness at the moment as if the universe itself had paused to listen. As I scribbled down my thoughts, something profound came to me. I wrote, almost without thinking, "I have conquered my fear of death."

It was as though the words had materialised on the page before I fully grasped their meaning. But as I stared at them, I realised just how true they were. For so long, I had been caught up in mourning what I had lost—the life I once had, the person I used to be. That fear of death, both literal and figurative, had haunted me. I was afraid of losing my identity, of never being able to return to the person I thought I was meant to be.

But in that quiet moment, under the stars, I felt a sense of liberation. I had come to understand that life wasn't about clinging to the past or fearing the future. Life was happening *right now*, in this very moment. And I was still here, still breathing, still alive.

Reflection

That evening marked a turning point for me. I began to embrace each moment as an opportunity—a chance to start anew, to experience something fresh, to be fully present. For too long, I had been focused on what I had lost, but now I realised that life was offering me something even more precious: the present moment.

This shift in perspective filled me with a deep sense of gratitude. I started to notice the beauty in the ordinary, in the small things that had once seemed insignificant. The sound of birds chirping in the morning, the warmth of the sun on my skin, the way the leaves rustled in the wind—these simple moments became sources of joy. I found myself appreciating the little things I had once taken for granted.

I also started to let go of the pressure to constantly achieve or prove myself. I no longer felt the need to meet some external standard of success. Instead, I focused on being fully present, on enjoying the journey rather than obsessing over the destination. I realised that life isn't about reaching some ultimate goal; it's about experiencing each step along the way.

Lesson

The greatest lesson I learned during this time was that life is a series of moments to be cherished. We often get so caught up in the past, in our regrets or the things we wish we could change, that we forget to appreciate what's right in front of us. Similarly, we worry about the future, about what might happen, and in doing so, we lose sight of the present.

But the current moment is all we have. It is where life unfolds. By accepting the present now, we open ourselves up to the beauty and joy that may be found in even the tiniest of situations. We realise that life isn't about spectacular moments or big accomplishments—it's about the tiny things, the fleeting moments of connection, laughter, and love.

I learned that we don't need to have everything figured out. Life is unpredictable, and that's okay. There is beauty in the unknown, in the mystery of what each new day might bring. Instead of fearing the uncertainty, we can choose to embrace it, knowing that whatever happens, we have the strength and resilience to face it.

This realisation didn't come overnight, and it wasn't always easy to maintain. There were still moments when the fear and doubt crept in when I wondered if I would ever fully recover. But I had learned to anchor myself in the present, to remind myself that I didn't need to have all the answers right now. All I needed to do was take things one moment at a time, and trust that everything else would fall into place.

You know...

Embracing the unknown is not about giving up or resigning ourselves to fate. It's about recognising that life is full of surprises, both good and bad and that we have the power to choose how we respond to them. By focusing on the present and finding joy in the small things, we can live more fully, and more authentically.

In my journey of recovery, I discovered that life isn't defined by the obstacles we face, but by how we choose to overcome them. And in doing so, I found a sense of peace that I had never known before. The fear of death, of failure, of not being enough—all of it faded into the background, replaced by a deep appreciation for the here and now.

We all can embrace the present, let go of our fears, and find beauty in the everyday. It's a choice we can make, one moment at a time. And when we do, we unlock the true power of living—not just surviving but thriving in the face of whatever life throws our way.

7
The Power of Connection

As I navigated through my recovery, I learned that life's true strength lies in the connections we make with others. Throughout my journey, I encountered individuals who were fighting their own battles, each one teaching me valuable lessons about resilience, courage, and the power of community. One of the most profound moments came when I unexpectedly reconnected with a dear friend of mine.

Anecdote

We found ourselves in a cozy café, the aroma of freshly brewed coffee enveloping us like a warm hug. My friend, who had faced significant challenges of her own, greeted me with a radiant smile that immediately lifted my spirits. Over steaming mugs, we shared stories of our struggles and triumphs, each word weaving a bond between us.

At one point, she quoted Chris Brookes: "Having Down syndrome is like being born normal. I'm just like you, and you are just like me." These words struck me like a bolt of lightning. In that moment, I was reminded that we are all unique yet beautifully similar in our humanity. Her laughter was infectious, and the way she embraced life, despite the hurdles she faced, shifted my understanding of what it meant to be "normal."

I realised that the essence of life lies in our differences and that diversity is what makes our world vibrant. It became clear to me that I wasn't alone in my struggles; I had a friend who understood the depths of hardship but still found reasons to celebrate life. This close friend I'm referring here's name is **Reem**. Nationality, religion, nothing have any boundaries between real friends.

Reflection

These connections became my lifeline, and with each conversation, I felt the weight of isolation begin to lift. My friend's perspective encouraged me to reach out to others who had also faced their battles. I began forming new friendships, nurturing the existing ones, and weaving a tapestry of support around me.

The power of these relationships was transformative. I learned that sharing experiences, both joyful and painful, creates a sense of belonging that is invaluable. There were moments when I felt overwhelmed, and those friends stood by my side, reminding me that it was okay to be vulnerable. We laughed together, cried together, and celebrated each small victory as if it were a monumental achievement.

With each connection I forged, I discovered that everyone carries their own story of resilience and that every story holds the potential to inspire and uplift. I was no longer just a survivor of my circumstances; I was a part of a larger community of individuals who were bravely facing their challenges, too.

You know...

The most significant lesson that life has taught me during this period was that building connections fosters resilience. We are indeed stronger together. In a world that often feels isolating, the act of reaching out and forming bonds with others creates a safety net of support. It is a reminder that we don't have to face our battles alone.

Sharing our experiences—whether they are filled with joy or laced with pain—allows us to heal collectively. It diminishes the sense of isolation that can suffocate us in our darkest moments. The more we share, the more we realise that we all have fears, insecurities, and dreams.

Life's challenges are often unpredictable, but the relationships we build can provide the strength we need to navigate them. I learned to cherish these connections and to appreciate the unique stories that each person brings to the table.

In closing, I urge everyone to open their hearts and minds to the people around them. Don't shy away from reaching out, sharing your story, or listening to others. We are all in this together, navigating the complexities of life, and it is through these connections that we find not only solace but also empowerment.

As I continue on my journey, I carry with me the understanding that every interaction is a thread in the beautiful tapestry of life. Each thread, no matter how small, contributes to a larger picture filled with colour, depth, and meaning. So let us embrace our shared humanity and lift one another, for it is in the power of connection that we truly thrive.

8
Embracing Risks and Mistakes

Throughout my journey of recovery and rediscovery, embracing risks emerged as a central theme of my life. I began to learn that mistakes are not failures; rather, they are stepping stones on the route to growth. It was through taking risks that I truly learned what it meant to live fully.

Anecdote

One day, as I sought new ways to challenge myself, I stumbled upon an opportunity to join a college drama group. Despite my love for storytelling, I had never acted before, and the thought of stepping onto a stage was thrilling and terrifying. Nonetheless, I decided to leap into the unknown.

The initial rehearsal was a daunting affair. As I walked into the room, it was filled with both experienced actors and excited beginners. The environment was alive with excitement, and the group's camaraderie instantly became palpable. Although my heart was racing, I felt a spark of courage ignite within me. We started reading through the script, and despite my initial anxieties, I found that the shared laughter and encouragement from my other cast members fuelled my drive to overcome my phobia.

With each rehearsal, I found my footing, and performing became a celebration of resilience. I cherished the moments when we all came together, supporting one another through the ups and downs of the creative process. It was exhilarating to share the stage, to be part of something larger than myself.

Reflection

Then came the night of our first performance. The excitement was palpable, but anxiety tugged at my heart. Halfway through the play, in a moment of panic, I forgot my lines. My mind went blank, and for a brief second, I felt the weight of embarrassment wash over me. But instead of freezing, I improvised. I turned my blunder into a humorous exchange with my scene partner. The audience erupted with laughter, and I felt a rush of relief and exhilaration.

At that moment, I realised something profound: imperfection could be a source of joy. What initially felt like a disaster transformed into a highlight of the show. Embracing that mistake not only lightened the atmosphere but also brought a deeper connection between me and the audience. They were not there to see a perfect performance; they were there to share an experience with us, flaws and all.

You know that...

This experience taught me that taking risks is essential for personal growth. Each misstep provides valuable lessons that shape our journey, revealing strengths we didn't know we had. I learned that the fear of failure often holds us back from experiencing the fullness of life. By allowing myself to step outside my comfort zone, I discovered new passions and forged deeper connections with others.

As I reflect on my journey, I am reminded that the road to self-discovery is paved with challenges and uncertainties. Embracing risks is not just about seeking thrills; it's about having the courage to try new things, confront our fears, and understand that mistakes are simply part of the process.

So, I encourage everyone to step boldly into the unknown. Whether it's joining a new group, taking a class, or pursuing a dream, remember that every risk taken is a chance to grow. Embrace your mistakes, for they may lead to unexpected rewards and a richer, more vibrant life. We are all learners in this journey, and each experience, no matter how imperfect, adds a beautiful brushstroke to the masterpiece that is our life.

9

Finding Purpose

As I navigated my path of recovery and self-discovery, I stumbled upon a profound passion: helping others. Volunteering at a local support group became a cornerstone of my newfound purpose, a journey that began during my bachelor's degree program called "Sahaya." The initiative was intended to assist persons suffering from difficulties, and it opened my heart in ways I never expected.

Anecdote

During one memorable session, I had the opportunity to share my story with the group. I spoke candidly about my journey—my struggles, fears, and triumphs. As I looked around the room, I noticed the empathy reflected in the eyes of my listeners. It was a humbling experience to feel so seen and understood. Afterward, one participant approached me, tears glistening in their eyes. They thanked me for my honesty, sharing that my story resonated deeply with them and gave them the courage to face their challenges. This simple act of connection was powerful; it reinforced my belief in the incredible strength found in vulnerability.

Reflection

Through my volunteer work, I discovered that opening up creates a safe space for others to share their struggles. It became clear that vulnerability was not a weakness, but rather a bridge that connects us as human beings. In our group, we formed a community rooted in understanding and support, where everyone felt valued and heard. Each story shared was a testament to the resilience of the human spirit. As we listened to one another, we began to heal together, transforming our pain into a source of collective strength.

In those moments, I realised how crucial it is to allow ourselves to be vulnerable. It is often in our darkest times that we find the light of connection. I began to appreciate that sharing our stories not only empowers us but also creates an environment where others can feel safe to express their truths.

Consider that the lesson I learned was profound: vulnerability fosters connection and strength. When we share our experiences, we dismantle the walls that separate us. We cultivate empathy and compassion, reminding one another that we are never truly alone in our struggles. Each person we encounter carries their battles, and by embracing our vulnerabilities, we create a tapestry of shared experiences that uplifts and empowers us all.

As my journey progressed, I felt a newfound sense of purpose in helping others. I understood that every interaction, every shared story, has the potential to spark hope and healing. Life is not merely about our journeys; it is about the connections we forge along the way. In opening our hearts to one another, we not only find our strength but also inspire others to embrace their own stories. In this beautiful dance of vulnerability, we discover our true purpose: to support, uplift, and empower one another in this shared experience called life.

10
Lessons in Resilience

As I reflect on my journey, I have come to embrace a profound truth: resilience is not just about enduring hardship; it is about growing through it. Life has thrown its share of challenges at me, and each one has shaped who I am today.

Anecdote

I remember a particularly challenging week when everything seemed to go wrong. Multiple setbacks left me feeling overwhelmed. Instead of succumbing to despair, I decided to approach these obstacles differently. I picked up my journal and began to write about each encounter, carefully detailing what had happened and the lessons I could extract from them. One setback was a missed opportunity that left me disheartened, yet as I wrote, I realised that it opened the door to something even better. By the end of that week, I had transformed my frustrations into valuable insights that fuelled my growth.

Reflection

This experience taught me that my story was not just about the struggles I faced but also about the strength of the human spirit. I learned to view each challenge as a chance to learn something new. Instead of seeing setbacks as roadblocks, I recognised them as stepping stones that could lead me to greater understanding and resilience. Even the most daunting trials could be reframed as opportunities for personal evolution.

Know that

The lesson I hold close to my heart is that resilience is a journey, not a destination. It is about embracing challenges and recognising them for what they are: growth opportunities. Each moment of hardship has the potential to teach us something invaluable about ourselves and the world around us. I now understand that by learning from these experiences, we allow ourselves to evolve, becoming stronger and wiser along the way. Life may not always go as planned, but it is through our resilience that we find our true selves. This second chance at life has given me the wisdom to embrace every challenge and cherish the lessons they bring.

11
The Joy of Every Day

As the days unfolded, I began to discover a renewed sense of joy in the simple moments that life offers. After all that I had been through, I learned to appreciate the beauty that often goes unnoticed in the rush of everyday life.

Anecdote

One specific morning stands out strongly in my mind. I settled into my favourite chair with a warm cup of coffee in hand. As I took that first sip, I closed my eyes and inhaled the rich aroma. The warmth of the mug felt comforting against my palms, and I allowed myself a moment of serenity. In that stillness, it hit me just how often I rushed through these small experiences, glossing over the exquisite details of the ordinary. I had been so focused on the bigger picture that I had missed the joy hidden in each day. That morning, I vowed to change my approach.

Reflection

Embracing this shift in perspective allowed me to see each day as a new opportunity, a blank canvas waiting to be filled with colors of gratitude and wonder. I adopted the philosophy that "every day is a new life for a wise man," a mantra that became my guiding light. With this mindset, I started noticing the little things—a child's laughter, the rustling leaves, or even the sound of rain against my window. Each moment became a reason to celebrate life.

My lesson in this chapter of life...

What I learned through this transformation is profound: every day holds the potential for joy, no matter how small or mundane it may seem. When we take the time to embrace the beauty in ordinary moments, we enrich our lives in ways we never thought possible. This second chance at life has taught me that happiness often lies in the simplest of experiences. By being present and appreciating the little things, I have cultivated a deeper sense of fulfilment and joy, reminding myself that every day is indeed a precious gift.

12
The Future Unmapped

As I gaze toward the horizon of my future, I am filled with an exhilarating sense of hope and excitement. Life is like an unmapped road, brimming with endless possibilities and adventures waiting to unfold. This realisation is simultaneously liberating and motivating.

Anecdote

One evening, I found myself standing on a hill overlooking the city, with the bright colours of the sunset painting the sky in orange, pink, and gold. The world below me felt alive, and I was filled with a sensation of possibility. The beauty of the sunset reminded me that, like the colours of the sky, my future could be whatever I wanted it to be. I felt prepared to face whatever came next, my heart open to new experiences, and my mind devoid of dread.

Reflection

While uncertainty can often feel daunting, I've come to understand that it also holds the promise of growth and transformation. The unknown can be intimidating; it challenges us to step outside our comfort zones. But in doing so, we discover aspects of ourselves we never knew existed. "Life is either a daring adventure or nothing at all," Helen Keller once said. Each new chapter in my life has the potential for discovery, leading me to uncover hidden strengths and passions. The unpredictability of life teaches us to adapt and grow, pushing us toward becoming the best versions of ourselves.

KNOW THAT

I've learned to embrace the unknown wholeheartedly. Life's unpredictable nature is what makes it beautiful and transformational. Every twist and turn is an opportunity to learn something new, live life more fully, and connect with people in profound ways. I prefer to see what is ahead as a thrilling journey where I am the creator of my own story, instead of being afraid of it —one where I am the author of my own story.

As I move forward, I hold onto the belief that each day is a blank page, waiting for me to fill it with my choices, my dreams, and my courage. With every step I take into the future, I embrace the idea that the best is yet to come. The road may be unmapped, but I have faith in the journey ahead.

13

A Message to Others

As I stand here, reflecting on my journey, I feel an overwhelming urge to share my story, not just as a narrative of survival but as a beacon of hope. My message is simple: Embrace your adventures. Life's trials are not meant to break us; they are the very things that mold us into stronger, more resilient individuals. We are all capable of rising from the ashes of our struggles, and it is through this rise that we find our true selves.

Anecdote

Let me take you back to a day that still resonates deeply within me. After a speaking engagement, where I poured my heart out to an audience filled with eager faces, a young woman approached me with tears in her eyes. Her presence was filled with a mix of apprehension and hope. She shared her own story of struggle, recounting how life had thrown her curveballs she never anticipated. As she spoke, I was struck by her vulnerability—there was a raw honesty in her words that reminded me of my battles.

At that moment, I understood the power we hold when we share our experiences. Her words echoed back to me, illuminating the path of connection between us. I realised that in our vulnerability, we find strength, and in our struggles, we create a community that uplifts one another. We may feel isolated in our pain, but sharing our stories creates bonds that remind us we are never truly alone.

Reflection

To everyone reading this, I want you to know that embracing risks and making mistakes is not a sign of weakness but rather an essential part of growth. Each misstep is an opportunity to learn, to grow, and to develop a deeper understanding of ourselves. Life will challenge you; it will test your limits. But it is in facing these challenges that we find courage.

Pain can nurture bravery. It's the moments that bring us to our knees that ultimately teach us how to stand tall again. Each challenge we face is a chance to redefine our boundaries, to stretch beyond what we thought was possible. I encourage you to lean into discomfort, embrace uncertainty, and recognise that every moment of struggle can lead to profound transformation.

Lesson

Life continually offers significant changes, each a potential second chance. It is often in these moments of uncertainty that the greatest opportunities lie. Whether it's a career shift, a new relationship, or a change in perspective, every new beginning is a blank canvas, waiting for you to paint your story. Embrace these moments; let them shape your journey.

Never forget that your story matters. Your struggles, your triumphs, and your growth can inspire others to take that leap of faith. When you step into the light of your narrative, you encourage others to do the same. Your voice has the power to uplift and inspire, to create a ripple effect that reaches far beyond your own experience.

Here's the share of my MESSAGE....

I invite you to join me in this journey of embracing life's adventures. Together, let's cultivate a spirit of resilience and compassion. Let's remind one another that we are all in this together, navigating the unpredictable waters of life. When we share our stories, we create a tapestry of experiences that enrich our lives and the lives of those around us.

In closing, I leave you with this thought: "Your past does not define you; it refines you." Every trial, every setback, is a stepping stone toward the person you are meant to become. Embrace your journey, and let your story be the guiding light for others who are navigating their paths. Together, we can build a community rooted in strength, resilience, and unwavering hope. I am grateful that you allowed me to tell you about my journey.

14

The Excursionist's Legacy

As I stand at the crossroads of my life, navigating this unmapped road, I find myself immersed in the profound realisation that every experience we encounter shapes who we are. Life is a tapestry woven from our choices, our challenges, and our triumphs. Each thread, no matter how small or seemingly insignificant, contributes to the larger picture of our existence. My journey has taught me the invaluable lessons of resilience, connection, and authenticity. It is through these lessons that I hope to leave a legacy not just for myself but for those who walk alongside me on this unpredictable journey.

Anecdote

During a recent volunteer event, surrounded by a diverse group of individuals united by a common purpose, I found myself reflecting on the countless people I've encountered along the way. As we worked together to provide support and companionship to those in need, I listened intently to their stories—each tale uniquely beautiful yet eerily familiar.

One young man spoke of his struggles with mental health, recounting the dark days that seemed to swallow him whole. His words resonated deeply with me; I could see pieces of my journey reflected in his. Another woman shared her experiences of loss and heartbreak, illuminating the power of hope that can emerge from the depths of despair. In that moment, I was reminded of our shared humanity, a thread that connects us all regardless of our backgrounds or experiences.

In every conversation, I felt a deepening sense of empathy. Each person's story added depth to my own, reinforcing the notion that we are not alone in our struggles. We are all excursionists, navigating the winding paths of life, learning from one another as we forge ahead. It is this shared experience that creates a bond, a tapestry of connection that enriches our lives and strengthens our resolve.

Reflection

I take great pride in being an excursionist, in forging my path in a world that often seeks to define us. Society has a way of placing labels on individuals, creating expectations that can feel suffocating. But I refuse to be confined by those definitions.I am a unique combination of my experiences, dreams, and ambitions. I welcome the unpredictable nature of my journey, understanding that every twist and turn presents a chance for progress.

Let my story be a reminder that we all have the power to overcome adversity. Our journeys may be fraught with challenges, but it is within those challenges that we discover our true strength. As I reflect on my trials, I recognize that each obstacle has been a stepping stone toward becoming the person I am today. The scars I carry are not symbols of defeat; they are badges of honor that tell the story of my resilience.

In the words of a personal mantra, I often remind myself: **"Every setback is a setup for a comeback."** Life may knock us down, but it is our response that truly defines us. With every challenge face,

I choose to rise, learn, and grow. It is this unwavering spirit that transforms adversity into a powerful catalyst for change.

Lesson

As I continue my journey, I urge you to embrace your unmapped road. Life is not merely about reaching a destination; it is about cherishing each moment along the way. The journey is just as important, if not more so, than the end goal. Every step holds meaning, every experience contributes to your growth.

Remember, ***"In the journey of life, it is not the miles traveled that matter, but the moments that take our breath away."*** Seek out those moments, for they are the treasures that will stay with you long after the journey is over. Embrace the beauty of the unknown and the power of exploration.

As we walk our paths, let us carry forward the legacies of resilience, connection, and authenticity. Share your story, just as I share mine, and in doing so, create a ripple effect of inspiration. You never know who might be listening, who might find solace in your words, or who might be inspired to take their courageous steps forward.

In closing, let us not forget the power of our journeys. Each experience, each encounter, and each lesson learned shapes who we are and who we will become. May we all embrace our roles as excursionists, navigating this beautiful, chaotic life with courage, grace, and an open heart. As we journey onward, let us remember: ***"The legacy we leave is not in the places we visit, but in the hearts we touch along the way."*** So go forth, dear friends, and make your mark on the world.

Conclusion: Embrace The Journey

As I close this chapter of my life, I am filled with a profound sense of gratitude and reflection. Each twist and turn, every challenge and triumph, has contributed to the tapestry of who I am today. I have learned that life is not merely about the destination we seek, but the richness of the journey we undertake to get there. It is a continuous evolution of self, a path marked by resilience, growth, and unwavering hope.

Recently, I found myself revisiting the park where, not so long ago, I felt completely lost. Memories of that place flooded back—the weight of uncertainty and fear that had once consumed me. But this time, as I stepped onto the familiar path, something remarkable had changed. I walked with my head held high, feeling the warmth of the sun on my face, and I embraced the beauty of my journey. I realised I no longer saw the park as a symbol of my past struggles but as a sanctuary of strength and transformation. Each blade of grass and rustling leaf echoed the stories of resilience that have shaped my heart.

In those moments of quiet reflection, I understood that every obstacle I faced was not a hindrance but a stepping stone, guiding me toward becoming a better person. The pain I endured taught me empathy; the challenges I overcame fostered strength; and the moments of vulnerability I embraced revealed the power of connection. I am grateful for every moment, every difficulty, and every triumph that has moulded my spirit.

The road ahead may be unpredictable, filled with unknowns and surprises, but I stand ready to face it all with courage and joy. I am armed with the knowledge that I am not alone; I am part of a community of excursionists, each navigating their unique paths. Together, we can share our experiences and uplift one another as we traverse this beautiful and chaotic life.

Let this be an invitation to you, my dear reader. Allow yourself to join me in celebrating the beauty of resiliency and the strength of the human spirit. Let us stroll down our uncharted paths, turning problems into possibilities and discovering the remarkable within the everyday. Life's moments, both big and small, hold the potential for greatness. In the simplest of joys—a warm cup of coffee, the laughter of friends, the vibrant colours of a sunset—we can find reminders of the beauty that surrounds us.

As we continue to embrace the journey, let us remain open to learning, growing, and evolving. May we find strength in our struggles, purpose in our passions, and connection in our shared stories. In doing so, we create a legacy of hope and inspiration for ourselves and those who come after us.

I can't miss pointing this out, "Pappa, you, the pillar of my strength, are the man who showed me how to be strong, independent, and fearless. No words are enough to express how grateful I am for being your daughter, who you never give up on teaching for being the best human possible."

In closing, remember this: "Every moment is a chance to rewrite your story." No matter where you are on your journey, you have the power to transform your life. Embrace it. Celebrate it. Live it fully. And as you navigate your path, know that the best is yet to come

- EXCRUSIONIST

Synopsis

" The Excursionist of an unmapped road " is an inspiring journey of resilience and self-discovery. Raised in a loving and supportive environment, the author seemed destined for success—excelling in school, sports, and becoming a role model admired by many. But a sudden, life-altering accident shattered that world, leaving everything unrecognisable. Faced with physical and cognitive challenges, the path to recovery was anything but straightforward. Through determination, perseverance, and the power of human connection, the author learned that life's greatest lessons come from adversity. This book is a powerful testament to finding strength in the face of hardship and turning setbacks into opportunities for growth. Discover the transformative power of resilience and the beauty of becoming the best version of yourself.

Author: Suha